GETTING STARTED

FREDDIE NORTH
Foreword by BOBBY WOLFF

HOW TO PLAY BRIDGE

NTC
NTC Publishing Group
NTC/Contemporary Publishing Company

Library of Congress Cataloging-in-Publication Data is on file at the United States Library of Congress

Published by NTC Publishing Group
An imprint of NTC/Contemporary Publishing Company

Printed in Singapore
International Standard Book Number:
0-8442-2563-0

contents

foreword

Bridge is a game enjoyed by many millions of players all over the world.

In these days of rising commercial pressures, increasing leisure and greater longevity, bridge has the potential to break down social and ethnic barriers and to keep the wheels of the brain turning in both the old and the young. Apart from that, bridge at whatever level is a very inexpensive game; all you need to play is a flat surface that the four players can sit round with a pack of cards and, of course, an understanding as to how to play the game.

It is for these reasons that I am particularly pleased to welcome the 'How to Play Bridge' series which has been specially designed to make the game easy to follow for beginners, no matter what their age. I believe that you will find the whole series well presented and particularly easy to read.

It is a curious fact, that over the years many of the great bridge authors have been British. Names like Victor Mollo, Hugh Kelsey, Skid Simon and Terence Reese still figure prominently in the USA lists of the greatest selling bridge books, so the fact that this series of books has been generated in Great Britain comes as no real surprise. I happen to know that all the authors have played bridge at International level so, in general terms, they should know what they are talking about. Furthermore, all of the books are based on the methods that are played all over the United States today. So, once you have learned, you should have little difficulty in getting a game whenever you want to.

I believe that after studying the 'How to Play Bridge' series you will not only be off to a good start, you will be totally enthralled by this great game.

Bobby Wolff
Dallas, Texas
March 1997

part one

introduction

So you want to learn to play this wonderful game and join the millions of others around the world who get such tremendous pleasure from it. That is a great decision and I am sure it is one that you'll never regret.

Bridge is easily the most exciting card game ever invented. It's fun to play, totally absorbing and embraced by the young and old alike. It's a game that enables you to meet people, make friends and is the complete antidote to loneliness and personal worries.

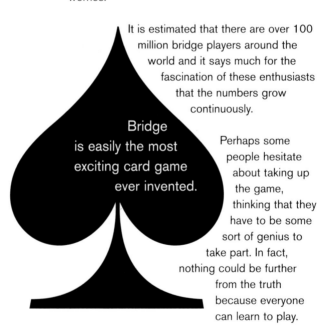

It is estimated that there are over 100 million bridge players around the world and it says much for the fascination of these enthusiasts that the numbers grow continuously.

Bridge is easily the most exciting card game ever invented.

Perhaps some people hesitate about taking up the game, thinking that they have to be some sort of genius to take part. In fact, nothing could be further from the truth because everyone can learn to play.

Another misconception is that you have to be a great mathematician. Nonsense! If you can count up to thirteen you're in business! What about a prodigious memory? Forget it. Just the ordinary memory that we all possess is quite enough.

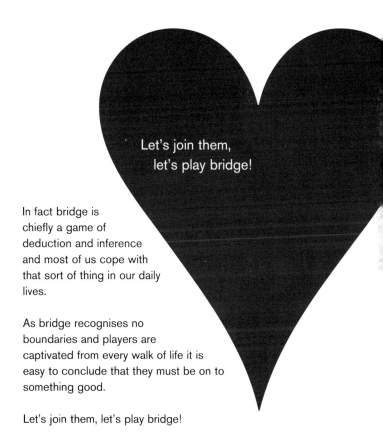

Let's join them,
let's play bridge!

In fact bridge is chiefly a game of deduction and inference and most of us cope with that sort of thing in our daily lives.

As bridge recognises no boundaries and players are captivated from every walk of life it is easy to conclude that they must be on to something good.

Let's join them, let's play bridge!

the players and the partnership

Starting right at the beginning then, we need four players who will form two partnerships. If the players have not already decided on the formation of the partnerships before arriving at the table (say, the Smiths v the Browns) then the partnerships are determined by drawing cards.

drawing for partners and the deal

All four players draw a card. The two highest play together leaving the two lowest to form the other partnership.

Bridge is played with two 'decks' of cards (one at a time) of contrasting colours. One of the players spreads a deck across the table and all four players draw a card. The two highest play together leaving the two lowest to form the other partnership. No player should draw a card adjoining one drawn by another player, or draw one of the four cards at the end of the deck. A card should not be exposed until all four players have drawn. The player with the highest card has the choice of seats and cards and deals first.

Suppose the four cards drawn are ♥A, ♦9, ♦3 and ♣4. Well, there is no problem. The ♥A and ♦9 play together and the player with the ♥A chooses the seats and cards and deals first.

But the situation is not so clear cut if the four cards happen to be something like this: ♠10, ♣9, ♥9, ♦6. The ♠10 is the highest card but who is his partner, the ♣9 or the ♥9? This is determined by the seniority of the suits.

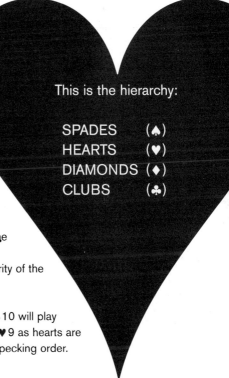

This is the hierarchy:

SPADES   (♠)
HEARTS   (♥)
DIAMONDS (♦)
CLUBS   (♣)

So the player with the ♠10 will play with the player with the ♥9 as hearts are higher than clubs in the pecking order.

the hierarchy:

SPADES	(♠)
HEARTS	(♥)
DIAMONDS	(♦)
CLUBS	(♣)

Your partner will sit opposite you and the other two – your opponents – will be on your left and right facing each other.

the shuffle

A little jingle that may help you to remember the correct side goes: *If you're not demented quite, place the cards upon your right*

The player on the dealer's left shuffles the selected deck thoroughly and then passes it to the dealer who may, if he wishes, give it a final shuffle. Meantime, the dealer's partner is shuffling the other deck. When satisfied he places it face down on his right ready for the next deal.

A little jingle that may help you to remember the correct side goes: If you're not demented quite, place the cards upon your right.

the cut

The dealer presents the shuffled deck to the opponent on his right who cuts it – usually somewhere in the middle but in any case each portion must contain at least four cards – towards the dealer so that the two portions are left on the table. The dealer completes the cut by placing the portion that was originally on the bottom of the deck on the top and then he prepares to deal.

The player to the right of the dealer cuts the pack.

the deal

The dealer distributes the cards face down one at a time to each player, starting with the player on his left and finishing with himself. Now each player has 13 cards. At the conclusion of each hand the deal passes in a clockwise direction so that each player deals in turn, always using the other deck that has been shuffled by the dealer's partner.

description of the deck

The honor cards are:

The Ace	(A)
The King	(K)
The Queen	(Q)
The Jack	(J)
The Ten	(10)

There are 52 cards in each deck consisting of four suits of 13 cards each. SPADES, HEARTS, DIAMONDS & CLUBS. Throw the jokers away – they play no part in the game. The honor cards are the AKQJ10. The ace, the king, the queen, the jack and the ten.

The ace wins over any other card in the suit and the king beats all other cards in the suit except the ace. At the other end of the scale, the two loses to all cards in the suit.

tricks

There are 13 tricks at stake. All four players must play a card to each trick, following suit if they can but otherwise discarding from another suit or playing a 'trump'. Following suit means playing a card from the suit that has been led. So, if the leader plays a diamond you must also play a diamond if you have one.

The player who wins the trick always leads to the next trick.

Provided that the trick is not 'trumped', the player who plays the highest card in the suit wins the trick. So, if the four cards comprising a trick are the four of diamonds, the seven of diamonds, the ten of diamonds and the queen of diamonds, the trick is won by the player who contributed the queen.

The player who wins the trick always leads to the next trick.

what is a trump?

Trumps are determined in the 'auction'. As we shall see, the auction will determine whether we play with clubs, diamonds, hearts or spades as trumps or whether we play with no trumps at all.

Even the lowest trump of all takes precedence over all other cards in another suit but, remember, you can't use a trump if you are able to follow to the suit that has been led.

So, suppose that diamonds have been led and hearts are trumps. If the other three players have played diamonds and you have no diamonds left, you can win the trick by playing any trump. Normally, you would win by playing your lowest trump. Even the two of hearts will be sufficient to win the trick in this case.

object of the game

Basically the idea is to take tricks – as many tricks as possible. Each partnership determines its combined strength and sets course accordingly.

> **Basically the idea is to take tricks – as many tricks as possible.**

This is done in the auction, or the bidding as it is often called. One side wins the auction, by bidding higher than the other side, and then has the task of fulfilling the contract. The side that wins the auction has to try and make the the number of tricks (or more) for which it has bid in the denomination chosen in the auction.

The opposing pair, now called the defenders, do all they can to prevent this.

So, for example, if the side that won the auction are trying to make nine tricks, the side that are defending must aim to take at least five tricks.

progress of the auction

Higher means higher in rank or number.

Each bid that is made must be higher than any previous bid (except for a double or redouble which are explained later).

Higher means higher in rank or number. Here again is the hierarchy with, this time, the addition of NO TRUMPS which heads the table.

NO TRUMPS
SPADES
HEARTS
DIAMONDS
CLUBS

So One Spade will outbid One Heart, but suppose you wish to introduce your club suit (over One Heart) then you must bid Two Clubs. Of course you do not have to bid at all in which case you say PASS.

One Spade will outbid One Heart

The auction ends following three passes, say:

West	North	East	South
Pass	Pass	1♣	1♦
1♥	3♦	Pass	Pass
Pass			

Note: A bid of 1 commits you to making 7 tricks (the first 6 are assumed), a bid of 2 = 8 tricks and so on. Thus a bid of 6 = 12 tricks (a small slam) and a bid of 7 = 13 tricks (a grand slam, all the tricks).

In the above bidding example, South is saddled with the task of making his contract (he is called the declarer) as he bid diamonds first. His main objective will be to win 9 tricks, any extras being a bonus. Of course, the opposition (the defenders) will do their utmost to win at least 5 tricks, to defeat declarer's contract.

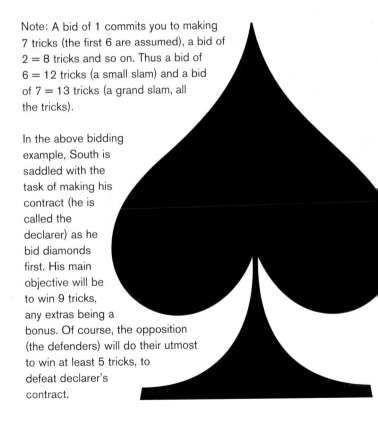

the play begins

When the auction is over, the player on declarer's left (remember, declarer is the player who is going to play the hand because he bid the trump suit, or no trumps, first and his side won the auction) leads a card and nothing can happen until that card is on the table.

The player on declarer's left is the player who makes the opening lead.

Once the lead is made (known as the opening lead), declarer's partner places his cards face upwards on the table, trumps on his right. His hand is called 'dummy' and he takes no further part in the play of the cards. It is now up to declarer to land his contract. Any extra tricks will count in the final score, but fulfilling the contract, i.e. not going down, is the essential task. You will probably find it a little confusing at first as you play not only your own cards but dummy's too, but this is something that you will soon get used to. Remember, if you win a trick in one hand you must play from that hand next.

This is without doubt the most difficult factor a novice declarer has to take on board. The good news is that eventually it becomes automatic.

Remember, if you win a trick in one hand you must play from that hand next.

play in a no trump contract

```
              ♠ A72
              ♥ 103
              ♦ KJ1094
              ♣ A103
  ♠ QJ1094      N        ♠ 863
  ♥ K95                  ♥ Q86
  ♦ 72       W     E     ♦ A83
  ♣ J87         S        ♣ Q1096
              ♠ K5
              ♥ AJ742
              ♦ Q65
              ♣ K52
```

Contract 3NT by South. Opening lead ♠Q.

When dummy goes down South
(declarer) counts his certain tricks. He
will then know how many more he
need establish and what plans
he should make to obtain them.

The ace and king of spades
plus the ace and king of
clubs and the ace of hearts
total five tricks. So four more
are required. Obviously dummy
has a nice source of tricks in the diamond
suit and taking the two hands

together (North's and South's) the only missing card that matters is the ace. Once this card is knocked out the diamond suit will be good for four tricks — just what is needed.

Remember:
Make a Plan
before you play
a card.

The plan then is quite simple. Win the spade lead in either hand, it really doesn't matter which one you choose, but let's say you win with the king. The queen of diamonds comes next and if the ace is held-up you continue diamonds until East takes his ace.

You win the next trick, no matter what East plays although it is likely to be a second spade, and collect your winners, i.e 2 spades, 4 diamonds, 2 clubs and 1 heart.

play in a suit contract

This time we play with a trump suit.

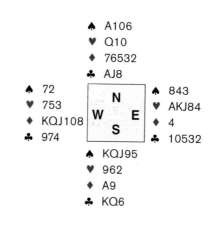

```
              ♠ A106
              ♥ Q10
              ♦ 76532
              ♣ AJ8
  ♠ 72                      ♠ 843
  ♥ 753         N           ♥ AKJ84
  ♦ KQJ108   W     E        ♦ 4
  ♣ 974         S           ♣ 10532
              ♠ KQJ95
              ♥ 962
              ♦ A9
              ♣ KQ6
```

Contract 4♠ by South. Opening lead ♦K.

In suit contracts it is often easier to count your losers.

In suit contracts it is often easier to count your losers and make your plan from there. In the present case declarer can see three losing hearts and one losing diamond. That's just one too many. However, one of the heart losers can be trumped in dummy providing that declarer delays drawing trumps until he has achieved his objective.

So the plan is this. Win the ace of diamonds and immediately give up a heart. Win the next trick and play a second heart. The scene is now set to trump the third heart in dummy, draw the opponents' trumps and then cash the three club winners. Declarer loses just two hearts and one diamond.

Declarer collects his own tricks and either defender – but only one of them – should be the custodian of the defensive tricks.

One little point to note. Each side should place their winning tricks in identifiable manner face down in front of them so that both parties can determine the number of tricks won and the order in which they were taken.

Declarer collects his own tricks and either defender – but only one of them – should be the custodian of the defensive tricks.

part two

scoring

There are three main ways of scoring points.

1. By winning a 'rubber' (two games of 100 points or more each)
2. By collecting penalties from the opponents when they fail in their contracts
3. By bidding and making slams (12 or 13 tricks)

There should be four score sheets on the table and each player ought to keep score. This is how the score sheet looks.

	We	They
	20	
(a)	40	120

(a) ... (b)

Everything you or they bid and make goes below the thick horizontal line (a). All other scores go above the thick horizontal line.

The main object is to make two games to win the rubber. A game (100 points or more) can be made on one hand or after several bites at the cherry. If you have a part-score and the opponents then make a game, a line (b) is drawn across both columns so that your part-score, although it counts in your grand total at the end, is no longer valid in helping towards your game – as in the example.

The main object is to make two games to win the rubber.

suit and no trump values

score for each trick
(in addition to the assumed six)

NO TRUMPS   40 for the first trick
NO TRUMPS   30 for each other trick

So if you bid 1NT and make 7 tricks, you score 40 points below the line.

If you bid 1NT and make 8 tricks, you score 40 points below the line and 30 bonus points for the 'overtrick' above the line. However, if you bid 2NT and make 8 tricks you score 70 points below the line.

Only points below the line count towards making a game.

Spades and Hearts are known as the majors

SPADES   (♠)   30 for each trick
HEARTS   (♥)   30 for each trick

Diamonds and Clubs are known as the minors

DIAMONDS   (♦)   20 for each trick
CLUBS   (♣)   20 for each trick

essential scoring

A game = 100 points or more

WHEN YOU HAVE MADE A GAME
YOU ARE 'VULNERABLE'.

Two games = rubber

When you have made a game, you are 'vulnerable'.

If you are looking for a game on one hand, as opposed to two or more partscores these are the contracts you should have in mind:

3 NO TRUMPS (40,30,30) = 100 (9 tricks)
4 SPADES or HEARTS (30) = 120 (10 tricks)
5 DIAMONDS or CLUBS (20) = 100 (11 tricks)

Most game contracts, successful on just one hand, are made in 3NT, 4♠ or 4♥.

the penalties for going down

	Not vul.	Doubled	Vul.	Doubled
1 Down	50	100	100	200
2 Down	100	300	200	500
3 Down	150	500	300	800
4 Down	200	800	400	1100

Each additional undertrick

Not vul.	Doubled	Vul.	Doubled
50	300	100	300

So, for going down when not vulnerable, providing that your contract is undoubled, you concede 50 points a trick that you fail by, and under the same conditions 100 points per trick when vulnerable.

Remember penalties mount up: if the final contract fails when doubled.

Of course the penalties mount up if the final contract fails when doubled. However, if you make your contract when doubled, your score is doubled and you get a bonus of 50 points.

Say you are doubled in Four Spades which is just made, your score is:

$$120 \text{ doubled} = 240 + 50 = 290.$$

The bid 'Double' takes the place of any other bid, as indeed does 'Redouble'.

In effect these bids just increase the stakes. If you think that you can beat the opponents' contract you can double, thereby substantially increasing the value of any penalty you might collect.

Of course, if he makes his contract (sometimes because your double warns him of the danger) he scores a bonus and if he really thinks you were mistaken to double he can up the ante by choosing to redouble.

The bid 'Double' takes the place of any other bid, as indeed does 'Redouble'.

If you make a redoubled contract, the score is exactly double the score for making a doubled contract.

So, Four Spades redoubled bid and made =

120 redoubled = 480 + 100 = 580

Similarly, if you fail in a redoubled contract, the penalty is twice the doubled penalty. For example, two down doubled vulnerable costs 500 points, while two down redoubled costs 1000 points.

If you make a redoubled contract, the score is exactly double the score for making a doubled contract.

slam bonuses

		Not vul.	Vul.
Small slam	(12 tricks)	500	750
Grand slam	(13 tricks)	1000	1500

honors

You score a bonus for your side for having four (out of the five) trump honors in one hand.

Five trump honors in one hand, or four aces at no trumps = 150.

This bonus = 100, whether you are the declarer or a defender. Five trump honors in one hand, or four aces at no trumps = 150.

rubber bonus

Winning a two game rubber	=	700
Winning a three game rubber	=	500

a completed score sheet

Here is a completed score sheet where 'We' finish
the rubber by bidding and making a small slam.

	We	They	
(i)	500		
(h)	750		
(e)	30		
(c)	200	200	(f)
(a)	30	50	(d)
(a)	60	100	(b)
(e)	120		
(g)	20		
(h)	190		
We	1900	350	
They	350		
Difference	1550		

50 or more counts as a complete 100 so 'We' win
by 16 points.

(a) We bid 2♠ and made 9 tricks
(b) They bid 3NT and just made it. That wiped out our partscore
(c) They went two down vulnerable
(d) We failed by 1 trick not vulnerable
(e) We bid 4♥ and made 11 tricks. 120 below the line and 30 above
(f) We went one down doubled vulnerable
(g) We bid and made 1♦
(h) We bid and made 6NT
(i) Rubber bonus, three game rubber

Remember:
It is only what you bid and make that goes towards your game.

Remember: It is only what you bid and make that goes towards your game. If you bid Two Hearts and make 11 tricks, only 60 goes below the line. The extra 90 goes with the bonus scores above the line.

part three

the bidding

how to evaluate your hand

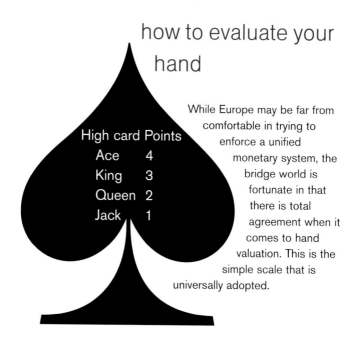

High card Points

Ace	4
King	3
Queen	2
Jack	1

While Europe may be far from comfortable in trying to enforce a unified monetary system, the bridge world is fortunate in that there is total agreement when it comes to hand valuation. This is the simple scale that is universally adopted.

high card points

So each suit has 10 H.C.P. and therefore there is a total of 40 H.C.P. in the pack. An average hand consists of 10 H.C.P.

Ace	4
King	3
Queen	2
Jack	1

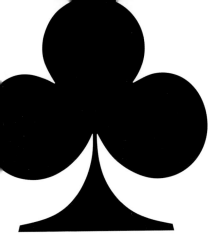

distributional points

Before going on to consider how many points are needed to open the bidding, there is one other factor that must be taken into consideration and that is DISTRIBUTION.

For the moment we are not concerned with the wild, exotic shapes but just the everyday hands boasting of five and six card suits. This is the distributional scale that should be added to your H.C.P. to help you determine whether or not you have an opening bid.

distributional points
Add 1 point for the fifth and 1 point for each extra card in the suit.

Add 1 point for the fifth and 1 point for each extra card in the suit.

critical number for opening the bidding

H.C.P. + D.P. = 13

You should always open with 13 points unless an opponent has opened in front of you.

The following hands constitute opening bids based on High Card Points + Distributional Points

You should always open with 13 points unless an opponent has opened in front of you.

1.

♠ AKJ86
♥ 743
♦ A62
♣ 94

12 H.C.P. + I D.P. = 13

2.

♠ 6
♥ KJ1094
♦ A10863
♣ K6

11 H.C.P. + 2 D.P. = 13

3.

♠ KQ9742
♥ 643
♦ 4
♣ AQ6

11 H.C.P. + 2 D.P. = 13

4.

♠ AK86
♥ 743
♦ A62
♣ Q75

13 H.C.P. + 0 D.P. = 13

5.

♠ AK86
♥ 7
♦ K642
♣ QJ53

13 H.C.P. + 0 D.P. = 13

6.

♠ KQJ10742
♥ 643
♦ 4
♣ A6

10 H.C.P. + 3 D.P. = 13

Note: We have added an extra point for the seventh card in the spade suit.

7.

♠ AQ104
♥ K75
♦ A42
♣ 986

13 H.C.P. + 0 D.P. = 13

Remember to count distributional points.

opening the bidding on minimum shapely hands

Length is more important than strength.

Length is more important than strength. After all, if you are going to suggest a trump suit to your partner it makes sense to indicate where you have plenty of them, not where they are in short supply.

If your partner responds in a different suit to the one in which you have opened the bidding, he will expect a rebid – unless he has already passed or you have an adequate part-score – so it is prudent to consider your rebid before opening.

Long suits of five and six cards can be rebid but you cannot rebid four card suits. Another thing to bear in mind is that minimum hands should be kept to minimum levels.

Long suits of five and six cards can be rebid but you cannot rebid four card suits.

That means the one or two level, and avoid allowing the bidding to

escalate to the three level or even higher. With this point in mind, you should open the higher of two touching five card suits and rebid the lower. (Touching means in the hierarchy of Spades – Hearts – Diamonds – Clubs.)

♠ Q10864
♥ AJ975
♦ AQ
♣ 4

Open One Spade, prepared to rebid Two Hearts over partner's response of two of a minor or One No Trump.

♠ 63
♥ J10865
♦ AKQ4
♣ K3

Open One Heart, prepared to rebid Two Diamonds. Length is more important than strength.

Remember: length is more important than strength.

♠ 4
♥ A10963
♦ AKJ94
♣ 73

Open One Heart, prepared to rebid Two
Diamonds. If partner prefers hearts he can put you
back to Two Hearts without increasing the level of
the bidding.

♠ –
♥ K62
♦ AJ1075
♣ AQ982

Open One Diamond, prepared to rebid Two Clubs.

With length in clubs and spades it is usually best
to open One Club as this facilitates your rebid.

♠ AJ1074
♥ 4
♦ 82
♣ AQJ63

With
length in
clubs and
spades it is
usually best to
open One Club

Open One Club, prepared to rebid
One Spade. If you open One Spade
and partner responds Two Diamonds or
Two Hearts, you will have an uncomfortable rebid.

With five spades and five diamonds or five hearts and five clubs it is generally best to open the major.

♠ AJ975
♥ Q3
♦ KJ974
♣ 4

Open One Spade, prepared to rebid Two Diamonds over Two Clubs or Two Spades over Two Hearts.

♠ 3
♥ A10864
♦ A3
♣ KQ963

Open One Heart, prepared to rebid Two Clubs over One Spade or Two Hearts over Two Diamonds.

With five spades and five diamonds or five hearts and five clubs it is generally best to open the major.

With five and four card suits that are not touching it is obviously correct to bid your five card suit first. Then, if at a convenient level, the four card suit can be bid next.

♠ AJ83
♥ 86
♦ AK1064
♣ 102

Open One Diamond, prepared to rebid One Spade over One Heart but Two Diamonds over Two Clubs.

♠ 64
♥ KQ1074
♦ J10
♣ AK53

Open One Heart, prepared to rebid Two Clubs over One Spade but Two Hearts over Two Diamonds.

With five and four card suits that are not touching it is correct to bid your five card suit first.

♠ AKJ106
♥ 6
♦ KQ108
♣ 432

Open One Spade, prepared to rebid Two
Diamonds over Two Clubs but Two Spades over
Two Hearts.

♠ 83
♥ AQ106
♦ 94
♣ AQ1064

Open One Club, prepared
to rebid One Heart
over One Diamond
but Two Clubs over
One Spade.

The Standard
American System is
based on five
card majors.

Because the Standard American System is based on five card majors, it is necessary to open all 4-4-4-1 hands with one of a minor. With a singleton diamond the opening should be One Club. In all other cases open One Diamond.

With a 4-4-4-1 shape, including a singleton diamond, open One Club.

♠ A1064
♥ A1083
♦ 6
♣ KQ62

Open One Club, prepared to rebid One Heart over One Diamond. If your partner responds with a major suit then, of course, you will support him.

♠ KQ53
♥ Q1074
♦ AK106
♣ 5

Open One Diamond, prepared to rebid Two No Trumps if your partner responds Two Clubs. As before, support partner's major suit should he bid one.

♠ 5
♥ KJ96
♦ AQ103
♣ KJ42

Open One Diamond, prepared to rebid 1NT over One Spade.

♠ QJ96
♥ 5
♦ AJ94
♣ KQ75

Open One Diamond prepared to rebid One Spade over One Heart.

opening the bidding on minimum balanced hands

Special treatment is sometimes required when opening minimum hands without a long suit. This may include starting with a three card minor suit.

♠ Q102
♥ A106
♦ K52
♣ A1063

There is no problem here. Open One Club, prepared to rebid One No Trump over any change of suit by partner.

♠ AJ96
♥ KQ5
♦ Q74
♣ J103

Since we need a minimum of five cards in a major suit before we can open it, this hand is best opened One Club. The rebid is One No Trump over One Heart or One Diamond.

♠ KJ96
♥ Q63
♦ A1074
♣ K8

Open One Diamond, prepared
to rebid One No Trump over
One Heart or Two No Trumps
over Two Clubs.

♠ A4
♥ AJ96
♦ Q53
♣ K1074

Open One Club, prepared to rebid One No Trump
over One Diamond or One Spade, raise a One
Heart response to Two Hearts.

♠ QJ96
♥ A1064
♦ 74
♣ AQ5

Open One Club, prepared to
rebid One No Trump over
One Diamond.

♠ QJ96
♥ A1064
♦ AQ5
♣ 74

Open One Diamond, prepared to support either
major suit or rebid Two No Trumps over Two
Clubs.

Remember: You never have a rebid problem when
you have four card support for partner's suit.
Just support him.

Remember:
You never have a
rebid problem when
you have four card
support for partner's
suit. Just support him.

targets

Keeping your main targets in mind is well worth a little study, especially knowing the requirements for game.

With a combined point holding of:

21-24	25-26	33-34
Part-Score	Game	Small Slam

If the game contract is the slightly unusual one of five of a minor then the requirements should be raised to 27-28.

Remember your targets.

It could be argued that although you know your own point count you have no way – as yet – of knowing partner's. But already you know that your partner will have 13+ points to open the bidding, so if he opens and you also have an opening bid the joint values will add up to 26 points and you should reach a game contract. Equally, if your partner opens and you hold 20 points you are in the slam zone.

responding to partner's opening bid of one of a suit

What are your bidding options?

	Your options:	Points required
1.	Pass with a bad hand (1♥ –Pass)	0-5
2.	Bid a suit at the one-level (1♦ –1♠)	6+
3.	Bid a new suit at the two-level (1♥ –2♦)	10+
4.	Respond 1NT when unable to show a suit (1♠ –1NT)	6-9
5.(a)	Single Raise of partner's major suit with 3 or 4-card support (1♥ –2♥)	6-9
5.(b)	Double Raise of partner's major suit with 3 or 4-card support (1♥ –3♥)	10-12

5.(c) Raise to game in partner's major 13-15
(1 ♥–4 ♥)

6. Bid 2NT
Before passing 13-15
(1 ♠–2NT)

After passing 11-12
(1 ♠–2NT)

7. Make a jump bid in a 16+
new suit, which is forcing to
game, with a good fit in
partner's suit or with a self-
supporting suit of your own,
e.g. AKJ1095 or AKQ1053
(1 ♠–3♣)

clarifying the options

1. Pass with a bad hand   0-5

If you have nothing, say nothing. There is no obligation to keep the bidding open.

However, there are some shapely five-point hands which warrant a bid. For example, your partner opens One Diamond and you hold:

       ♠   AJ1064
       ♥   6
       ♦   9732
       ♣   1064

Respond One Spade. Too much potential to pass.

If you have nothing say nothing.

Alternatively, you might hold the following:

       ♠   Q64
       ♥   J72
       ♦   643
       ♣   Q842

This is a bad 5 points and partner's opening bid should be passed.

2.   Bid a suit at the one-level   6+

Show a four-card major in preference to One No
Trump or responding at the two-level with modest
values.

♠ QJ96
♥ 73
♦ AJ
♣ 108642

Respond One Spade to an opening of One
Diamond or One Heart.

3.   Bid a suit at the two-level   10+

This is a bid that must be kept up to strength. A
minimum of 10 points are needed. The alternative,
without the requisite number of points, is One No
Trump.

♠ 105
♥ 86
♦ A932
♣ AQ1064

Respond Two Clubs to one of a
major, but without the ♣Q you
would bid One No Trump.

4. Respond 1NT when   6-9
    unable to show a suit

This is the utility response when you
have 6-9 points but cannot bid a
suit at the one-level and are not
good enough to introduce
a new suit at the two
level.

With
6-9 points
respond 1NT when
you are unable to to
show a suit.

♠ K6
♥ QJ
♦ 9642
♣ Q7542

Respond One No Trump to one
of a major, and you should bid the
same way with both the following
examples as well:

To respond
in a new suit at
the two-level a
minimum of 10 points
are needed.

♠ J6   ♠ 75
♥ 84   ♥ A4
♦ Q96   or   ♦ KJ753
♣ A97542   ♣ 10652

5. When a 5-3 or 4-4 fit is located in the majors, support partner immediately applying the Support Point Scale that is shown on page 69.

♠ 4		♠ J964
♥ A109		♥ J853
♦ Q10975	or	♦ A102
♣ J863		♣ 75

(7 HCP + 2 SP = 9)   (6 HCP + 2SP = 8)

Raise partner's One Heart opening to Two Hearts.

With 10-12 points make a 'limit' raise.

♠ 8		♠ 10
♥ KJ6		♥ Q1096
♦ A10974	or	♦ A10974
♣ J632		♣ Q103

(9 HCP + 2 SP = 11)   (8 HCP + 3SP = 11)

Raise partner's One Heart opening to Three Hearts.

When a 5-3 or 4-4 fit is located in the majors, support partner immediately applying the Support Point Scale

With 13-15 points raise partner's major to game.

♠ 86
♥ AJ76
♦ KQ75
♣ K52

(13 HCP + 2 SP = 15)

Raise partner's One Heart
opening to Four Hearts.

Your hand may still warrant
a raise to game, even
though you passed
originally, by virtue of Support
Points.

Your hand may still warrant a raise to game even though you passed originally.

♠ 6
♥ AQ94
♦ KQ842
♣ 1052

(11 HCP + 3 SP = 14)

Whether you have passed or not, you should raise
partner's One Heart opening to Four Hearts with
this hand.

limit bids

All raises in partner's suit are limit bids. If minimum opener does not need to bid again.

In effect, when you raise opener from one to two you are saying, 'I have some support for you, and would hope that you will make 8 tricks even if you are minimum. If you are very strong, however, we might make game'.

Raises in partner's suit are limit bids.

Similarly, if you raise opener from one to three you are saying, 'I have good support for you, and a fair hand, but not so much that I expect to make game unless you have something extra. Pass, if you are minimum, bid on with more'.

6. Bid 2NT

The response of Two No Trumps shows 13-15
points before passing and 11-12 after passing.

♠ AJ9
♥ Q6
♦ KJ94
♣ QJ73

When your partner opens
One Heart, respond Two No
Trumps which is a forcing to
game bid.

♠ AJ9
♥ 64
♦ KJ94
♣ Q873

Having passed originally, you should respond Two
No Trumps to partner's opening bid of One Heart.
This is a 'limit' bid.

7. A jump bid in a new suit shows a big hand and is unconditionally forcing to game at least. This bid should not be made with a two-suiter, or when you have a misfit with your partner unless you have a powerful self-supporting suit of your own.

♠ A
♥ AKJ106
♦ KQ104
♣ 742

Respond Two Hearts to partner's One Diamond.

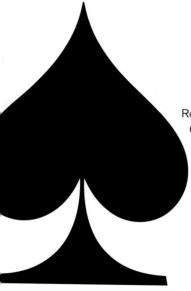

♠ AKQ10975
♥ 6
♦ 832
♣ AK

Respond Two Spades to partner's One Heart, One Diamond or One Club.

♠ 2
♥ AK1083
♦ AK1094
♣ K3

Respond Two Hearts to partner's One Spade.
When you show your diamonds later probably at
the three level your bid will be forcing.

The real reason for not jumping to
Three Hearts immediately with this
hand is that you need bidding
space to find out whether
you have a fit in
diamonds before the
bidding gets
uncomfortably
high.

If partner just
rebids his
spades you will
have to bid your
diamonds at the four-
level. If partner has no fit for either of
your suits this will take you past the
obvious stopping place of 3NT.
By responding Two
Hearts you will get the
opportunity to bid Three
Diamonds over Two Spades and then if
partner bids 3NT you can pass.

fitting hands

Since well-fitting hands plays so very much better than ill-fitting hands it is necessary to upgrade hands when a fit is located. Before examining the relevant scale, consider the following holdings in the heart suit.

1.	♥ AQ964	♥ 5
2.	♥ KJ975	♥ 63
3.	♥ KQ842	♥ 7
4.	♥ AQ964	♥ K1052
5.	♥ KJ975	♥ A863
6.	♥ KQ842	♥ AJ75

In examples 1, 2, and 3 there is no fit and establishing tricks is going to be uphill all the way.

However, in cases 4, 5, and 6, the suit knits together beautifully. Make it the trump suit and you are likely to have total control and considerable flexibility, ruffing (= trumping) in either hand at will.

Even ♥ AQ1075 opposite ♥ J94 offers considerable scope and on a good day will play for 5 tricks.

Support Points should be applied when a 4-4 or 5-3 fit is located – generally in the majors.

<blockquote>
Add Support Points when a 4-4 or 5-3 fit is located – generally in the majors.
</blockquote>

Add

For a void	3 points
For a singleton	2 points
For a doubleton	1 point

With a 9-card trump fit increase the scale by 1 point, i.e. 4–3–2. In particular, with 4-card support for a 5-card major suit opening apply the 4-3-2 Support Point Scale.

Suppose you pass, your partner opens One Heart and you hold:

1.

♠ 7
♥ Q1065
♦ A10852
♣ Q64

You are worth 8 HCP + 3 SP = 11 points.

Bid Three Hearts.

2.

♠ 10864
♥ A1074
♦ –
♣ 97432

You are worth 4 HCP + 4 SP = 8 points.

Bid Two Hearts.

3.

♠ –
♥ Q10742
♦ KQ852
♣ Q93

You are worth 9 HCP + 4 SP = 13 points.

Bid Four Hearts.

4.

♠ 64
♥ Q105
♦ K10863
♣ 9764

You are worth 5 HCP + I SP = 6 points.

Bid Two Hearts.

5.

♠ 62
♥ K96
♦ 74
♣ KQ10643

You are worth 8HCP + 2 SP= 10 points.

Bid Three Hearts.

You may wonder why this scale applies principally to the major suits. The reason is that with a fit in a minor suit it is often easier to make 9 tricks in No Trumps than eleven in the minor.

It is often easier to make 9 tricks in No Trumps than eleven in a minor.

Consider the following example:

♠ AK4
♥ 96
♦ AQJ95
♣ J64

♠ QJ
♥ KQ104
♦ K1084
♣ Q105

While Five Diamonds would stand little chance, Three No Trumps is virtually ironclad.

Playing in Five Diamonds you have to make 11 tricks but unfortunately the defense have three top winners, the ace of hearts and the ace and king of clubs.

Playing in 3NT, you have five top tricks in diamonds and three in spades and you must make at least one trick in either hearts or clubs.

part four

action

Now that we have completed the first stages of bidding let's look at eight more hands where the final contract is reached after a straightforward auction.

deal 1

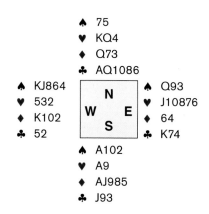

	♠ 75	
	♥ KQ4	
	♦ Q73	
	♣ AQ1086	

♠ KJ864   ♠ Q93
♥ 532   ♥ J10876
♦ K102   ♦ 64
♣ 52   ♣ K74

	♠ A102	
	♥ A9	
	♦ AJ985	
	♣ J93	

Final contract: 3NT. West leads the ♠6.

the bidding

South	West	North	East
1♦	Pass	2♣	Pass
2NT	Pass	3NT	Pass
Pass	Pass		

After South opens the bidding with 1 ♦, North knows that his side must reach game – an opening bid opposite an opening bid equals game – but he responds naturally (2♣) and awaits his partner's rebid. When South rebids 2NT there is little point in looking beyond 3NT for the final contract.

the play

West leads the six of spades and it is immediately clear that there are only six tricks on top:
1 spade,
3 hearts,
1 diamond
and 1 club.
However, the club suit offers considerable scope for developing the extra tricks as only the king is missing.

Count your top tricks.

If West has the king of clubs we can finesse him for it and probably make five tricks instead of one, and if East has it we can still make four tricks which will be enough for our contract.

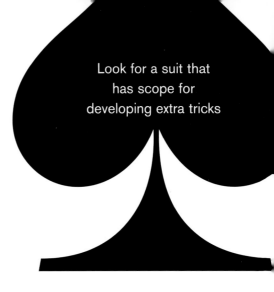

Look for a suit that
has scope for
developing extra tricks

There is one point that we should bear in mind. In case East has the king of clubs we should not win the ♠A until the third round so that communication between the defenders' hands is broken.

the play

The ♠Q is allowed to win and the spade continuation is won by West who plays a third spade to declarer's ace. Now the ♣9 is run to East's king (if East refuses the king on the first round, declarer continues with the jack which East must win). Declarer wins the next trick (probably the ♦A) and cashes his winners – the ♥AKQ and the remainder of the clubs, making exactly nine tricks.

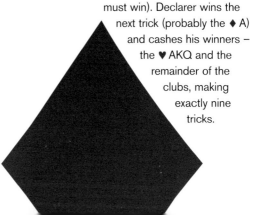

deal 2

The next hand was dealt like this:

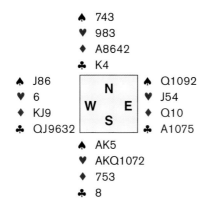

```
                    ♠  743
                    ♥  983
                    ♦  A8642
                    ♣  K4
    ♠  J86          ┌─────────┐      ♠  Q1092
    ♥  6            │    N    │      ♥  J54
    ♦  KJ9          │  W   E  │      ♦  Q10
    ♣  QJ9632       │    S    │      ♣  A1075
                    └─────────┘
                    ♠  AK5
                    ♥  AKQ1072
                    ♦  753
                    ♣  8
```

Final contract 4 ♥. West leads the ♣Q.

the bidding:

South	West	North	East
1 ♥	Pass	2 ♥	Pass
4 ♥	Pass	Pass	Pass

When North has enough to raise his partner's suit,
South quickly settles for a game in hearts making a
mental note that he must remember to claim his
100 honors at the end of the hand.

the play

West leads the ♣Q and when the king loses to the ace declarer sees that he may have four losers: 1 spade, 2 diamonds and 1 club. Still, there is that long diamond suit in dummy so maybe an extra trick can be established for a discard so long as East does not find an immediate spade switch.

The play goes like this. The club return at trick two is ruffed and trumps are drawn in three rounds. Then follows the key play, a small diamond from both hands. Perhaps East wins and switches to a spade but declarer wins and once again plays a low diamond from both hands. The defense win this trick and continue spades but declarer plays his master spade and leads a diamond to dummy's ace. The remaining two diamonds are now high. Declarer needs just one of them for a spade discard and can then claim the remainder of the tricks.

Remember to claim your bonus points for honors.

'We mustn't forget my 100 for honors as well, partner,' announces South with a triumphant smile as he writes down 120 below the line and 100 above.

deal 3

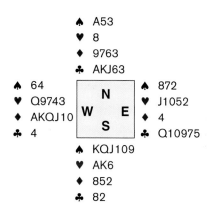

		♠ A53		
		♥ 8		
		♦ 9763		
		♣ AKJ63		
♠ 64				♠ 872
♥ Q9743		N		♥ J1052
♦ AKQJ10	W		E	♦ 4
♣ 4		S		♣ Q10975
		♠ KQJ109		
		♥ AK6		
		♦ 852		
		♣ 82		

Final contract: 4♠. West leads the ♦A.

the bidding

West	North	East	South
–	–	–	1♠
2♦	3♣	Pass	3♠
Pass	4♠	Pass	Pass
Pass			

> North's response of 3♣ over 2♦ is, of
> course, forcing and South can do no
> more than rebid his solid-looking spade

suit. North is then happy to raise to game and so the right contract is reached.

the play

West starts the attack with the four top diamonds, East following to the first round and then discarding three hearts. Declarer ruffs the fourth diamond, cashes the ♥A and has now arrived at the moment of truth. His small heart will be a loser unless he disposes of it. So he leads the ♥6 and ruffs in dummy … with the ♠A. He is then able to draw the outstanding trumps and claim the remainder of the tricks.

Had declarer made the mistake of ruffing in dummy with a small trump he would have been overruffed and his contract would have flown out of the window. The moral is simple. 'Don't send a boy on a man's errand.'

The moral is simple. 'Don't send a boy on a man's errand.'

deal 4

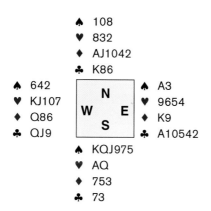

♠ 108
♥ 832
♦ AJ1042
♣ K86

♠ 642
♥ KJ107
♦ Q86
♣ QJ9

♠ A3
♥ 9654
♦ K9
♣ A10542

♠ KQJ975
♥ AQ
♦ 753
♣ 73

Final contract: 2♠. West leads the ♣Q.

the bidding

West	North	East	South
–	–	–	1♠
Pass	1NT	Pass	2♠
Pass	Pass	Pass	

North makes the courtesy response of 1NT to his
partner's opening bid 1♠ (he is not good
enough to bid 2♦) and South buys
the contract in 2♠.

the play

Since the ♣A is marked with East on the opening lead, the declarer observes that if the ♥K is also wrong he will have four losers outside the diamond suit (2 clubs, 1 heart and 1 spade). It will therefore be necessary to hold his diamond losers to one by taking a double finesse.

Anyway, the ♣K is taken by East's ace and a second club won by West. A third round of clubs is ruffed by declarer who now starts on trumps, dummy's ♠10 losing to East's ♠A. East switches to a heart and the queen loses to West's king. Declarer wins the next trick with the ♥A and draws the opponents trumps in two more rounds.

The time has now come to tackle the diamond suit. A small one is played towards the dummy and when West plays low the ten is played from dummy, losing to East's king. East continues with a third round of hearts which is ruffed by declarer. Now a second diamond is led towards dummy and when West plays low the jack wins the trick. So the declarer makes 5 spades, 1 heart and 2 diamonds, exactly fulfilling his contract.

All South asked of this hand was for at least one of the two missing diamond honors to be with West, or put another way – he didn't want East to hold both the king and queen. Not an unreasonable wish!

deal 5

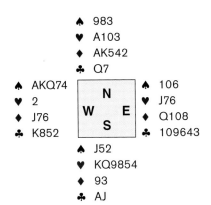

```
              ♠ 983
              ♥ A103
              ♦ AK542
              ♣ Q7
  ♠ AKQ74        N        ♠ 106
  ♥ 2                     ♥ J76
  ♦ J76      W     E      ♦ Q108
  ♣ K852        S         ♣ 109643
              ♠ J52
              ♥ KQ9854
              ♦ 93
              ♣ AJ
```

Final contract: 4♥. West leads the ♠A.

the bidding

West	North	East	South
1♠	Pass	Pass	2♥
Pass	4♥	Pass	Pass
Pass			

Although West opens the bidding East is unable to respond and North/South quickly get to their best game contract of 4♥.

the play

West cashes his top spades, East discarding the ♣3, and switches to the ♦6. Apart from the three spades, declarer sees that he is likely to lose a club trick as well, the king probably being with West to make up his values for an opening bid. However, before committing himself in clubs, the declarer plans to try and establish dummy's diamonds, but he must be careful to leave an entry in dummy (♥A) to enjoy the diamonds if in fact there is a favourable break.

So trick four is won with the ♦A and is followed by the ♥A, ♦K and a diamond ruff with the ♥9. When the diamonds fall 3-3 there is only one small hurdle left. Declarer must play a top heart from his own hand (just in case the outstanding hearts are divided 3-1) and then win the third round of hearts in dummy with the ace. There are now two winning diamonds in dummy but only one of them is required on which to discard the ♣J.

deal 6

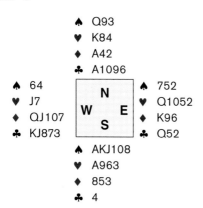

```
                    ♠ Q93
                    ♥ K84
                    ♦ A42
                    ♣ A1096
    ♠ 64              ┌─────────┐        ♠ 752
    ♥ J7              │    N    │        ♥ Q1052
    ♦ QJ107          │  W   E  │        ♦ K96
    ♣ KJ873          │    S    │        ♣ Q52
                      └─────────┘
                    ♠ AKJ108
                    ♥ A963
                    ♦ 853
                    ♣ 4
```

Final contract: 4♠. West leads the ♦ Q.

the bidding

West	North	East	South
–	1♣	Pass	1♠
Pass	1NT	Pass	3♥
Pass	3♠	Pass	4♠
Pass	Pass	Pass	

North's opening bid is music to South's ears
because it means that the partnership should reach,
and hopefully make, a game. Over South's natural
response of 1♠, North shows a minimum balanced
hand with 1NT, and since North could hold four
hearts South makes the forcing bid of 3♥ (2♥
might be passed). Dutifully, North gives preference

to 3♠ – obligatory with equal length in the two suits – and South continues to the spade game.

the play

West leads the ♦Q (top of a sequence is often best, as indeed it is here. It is also the unbid suit) and declarer notes that there would have been nine tricks on top had he let his partner play in 3NT. Still, if 4♠ makes it will score more, plus of course 100 for honors. The only snag is that there appear to be four losers: 2 diamonds and 2 hearts. The outstanding hearts could divide 3-3 (against the odds) in which case declarer's fourth heart would automatically become a winner.

However, declarer sees that it is unnecessary to rely on a 3-3 heart break. All he has to do is to ruff the fourth heart in dummy with a high trump before drawing all the trumps.

The play goes: ♦A, ♠A, ♥A, ♥K and concede a heart trick to East. The defense will take their two diamond winners but must then relinquish the lead so that declarer is able to ruff his heart loser in dummy as planned.

It should be noted that not more than one trump trick should be cashed initially. If declarer makes the mistake of cashing two top trumps immediately, East will play a third round when in with his heart trick and that would defeat the contract.

deal 7

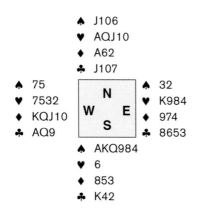

```
              ♠ J106
              ♥ AQJ10
              ♦ A62
              ♣ J107
  ♠ 75                        ♠ 32
  ♥ 7532         N            ♥ K984
  ♦ KQJ10    W     E          ♦ 974
  ♣ AQ9         S             ♣ 8653
              ♠ AKQ984
              ♥ 6
              ♦ 853
              ♣ K42
```

Final contract: 4♠. West leads the ♦K.

the bidding

West	North	East	South
–	1♣	Pass	1♠
Pass	1NT	Pass	4♠
Pass	Pass	Pass	

To give himself an easy rebid North opens 1♣ and then shows a modest balanced hand when he says 1NT. South then decides that he has heard enough and that 4♠ should be the safest game.

Superficially, there are four losers – just one too many – but declarer sees how he can utilise the heart suit so that one of those losers disappear – no matter who holds the king.

the play

The ♦A takes the first trick and is followed by the ♠A and then the ace and queen of hearts. If East plays the ♥K, South ruffs, draws trumps ending in dummy and discards his two losing diamonds on the ♥J10. This way he will eventually make eleven tricks, losing just two clubs.

If, on the other hand, East plays low on the ♥Q, declarer discards a losing diamond. West may win with the ♥K but will then only be able to cash one diamond; subsequently he will make a club trick but whether he takes it at once or waits until declarer has taken his discards on the ♥J10 – the result will be the same. The defense win three tricks and the declarer ten.

This play is called a Ruffing Finesse and the beauty of it is that the declarer must succeed no matter which opponent holds the missing king.

deal 8

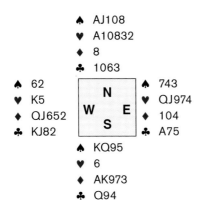

♠ AJ108
♥ A10832
♦ 8
♣ 1063

♠ 62
♥ K5
♦ QJ652
♣ KJ82

♠ 743
♥ QJ974
♦ 104
♣ A75

♠ KQ95
♥ 6
♦ AK973
♣ Q94

Final contract: 4♠. West leads the ♣2.

the bidding

West	North	East	South
–	–	–	1♦
Pass	1♥	Pass	1♠
Pass	3♠	Pass	4♠
Pass	Pass	Pass	

South opens his long suit (1♦) and North
responds in the same vein (1♥), but then the
spade fit is located and when North has the values

to jump to 3♠ (a limit bid) South is happy to bid game.

the play

West gets away to the best lead (♣2) and the defense soon muster the first three tricks, declarer's ♣Q being caught when East wins with the ace and returns his partner's suit.

West then switches to the ♠2 leaving declarer a lot of work to do. However, with singletons in each hand and high trumps with which to ruff declarer can count: 1 heart, 2 diamonds and 1 spade plus 3 ruffs in dummy and 3 ruffs in his own hand, making a grand total of ten tricks.

He has to be careful to cash the ♦AK before embarking on the cross-ruff, but the rest is plain sailing. The ♠8 wins trick four, then the ♦AK, diamond ruff, ♥A, heart ruff, diamond ruff, heart ruff, diamond ruff and finally a heart is ruffed with declarer's last trump.

This hand illustrates why it is so important to try and locate your 4-4 major suit fit.

glossary

Auction
The auction, which takes place initially, allows each player to bid in turn and so determine the final contract.

Balanced Hand
A hand in which the suits are evenly, or nearly evenly, distributed. 4-3-3-3, 4-4-3-2, or 5-3-3-2 are the hand patterns in the category.

Cashing
Cashing tricks means taking those that are there and available to be collected without having to resort to any special play.

Contract
The final bid, which is followed by three passes, becomes the contract. Making the contract is winning the number of tricks promised by the bid.

Cross-ruff
Trumping first in one hand and then in the other, usually between declarer and dummy but it can also be between the two defenders.

Cut
Before the deal commences, the player on the dealer's right must divide the deck by taking off a portion and placing it on the table towards the dealer. The dealer then completes the cut by placing what was originally the bottom portion on top of the other portion. Each portion must contain at least four cards to make it a legal cut.

Deal

The deal involves distributing the cards to each player in turn. The dealer starts with the player on his left and finishes with himself so that each player has thirteen cards.

Declarer

Declarer is the player whose responsibility it is to fulfil the contract. He has become declarer because he first bid the suit in which he is playing.

Defenders

The defenders are the pair opposing declarer and his dummy.

Distribution

How the cards are divided in a hand according to lengths and shortages – sometimes called shape.

Double

Takes the place of any other bid and, if left in, increases the penalty when the contract fails, but increases the amount won when the contract is successful. In some circumstances a Double is a conventional bid.

Doubleton

Just two cards only in a suit.

Down

When a player goes down he has failed to fulfil his contract and consequently has to concede a penalty.

Drawing Trumps

Taking the opponents' trumps away from them.

Ducking

Deliberately playing a low card when a higher one is available. The idea is that the high card(s) may be used to greater advantage later in the play.

Dummy

Dummy is declarer's partner who takes no part in the play of the hand. The dummy hand is the hand which is exposed on the table.

Entries

High cards or trumps that enable a player to reach his partner's hand.

Establishing

Making a suit good, either by ruffing the losers or conceding a trick or tricks to achieve the same purpose.

Finessing

Playing towards split honors in the hope of capturing the missing honor(s). e.g. lead small to AQ, AQ10, KJ, AJ10. But a finesse can be taken at much lower levels. e.g. lead small towards 108 hoping to find the 9 well placed.

Fit

When both partners have length in the same suit they have a fit. Say, AJ1084 opposite K973.

Forcing Bid

Any bid that compels partner to bid again. Sometimes referred to as a 'force'.

Game

100 points or more below the line.

Hold-up

Deliberately not taking a trick with a high card when one is available. See 'ducking'.

Honors

The honor cards are AKQJ10. When held in the trump suit they score 150 providing they are all in the same hand, or 100 for four out of the five in the same hand. All four aces in the same hand score 150 in no trumps.

Jump Bid

A bid that jumps a level. e.g. 1♣ – 2♥ or 1♠ – 3♦. Also called a jump shift.

Limit Bid

A bid that immediately limits the hand to within a narrow range, usually between 2 and 4 points.

Major Suits

Spades and Hearts.

Minor Suits

Diamonds and Clubs.

No Trumps

As the name implies, when playing in a no trump contract there are no trumps. The bid of no trumps ranks higher than any other bid at the same level thus it features immediately above spades.

Opening Lead

The original lead made by the defender on declarer's left.

Overcall

A bid made over an opponent's bid.

Overtricks

Tricks made over and above the number called, and scored above the line.

Part-score

A portion of the 100 points required for game.

Pass

The same as No Bid.

Penalty
Score conceded above the line for failing to make the contract.

Point Count
The almost universal method of hand valuation (Ace = 4, King = 3, Queen = 2, Jack = 1).

Raising
Supporting partners suit at a higher level.

Rebid
A second or later bid by a player who has already bid once.

Redouble
A double of a double. It doubles the penalties or the successful score again. It sometimes has a conventional meaning.

Revoking
Failing to follow suit when able to do so – for which there is a penalty.

Rubber
The best of three games.

Ruffing
Trumping when having none of the suit led.

Ruff & Sluff
Leading a suit in which dummy and declarer have none while they both still hold trumps. This enables declarer to ruff in one hand and discard a loser from the other.

Shape
The way the cards are distributed in a hand.

Shuffle
The mixing together of a deck of cards before the cut and deal takes place. This is carried out initially by the player on declarer's left.

Singleton

One card only in a suit.

Slams

Twelve winning tricks constitutes a Small Slam and all thirteen tricks, a Grand Slam.

Table

Playing from the table is synonymous with playing from dummy.

Targets

Something at which to aim depending on the combined values – Part-score, Game or Slam.

Tenace

Two cards in the same suit one of which is higher than the missing card and one lower. e.g. AQ, KJ, Q10, 108.

Touching Suits

The suits that come adjacent to one another in the hierarchy e.g. Spades and Hearts, Hearts and Diamonds, Diamonds and Clubs.

Tricks

Each player, in rotation, contributes a card and those four cards constitute a trick.

Trumps

The suit named in the final contract.

Void

Having no cards in one of the suits.

Vulnerable

When one partnership has scored a game it becomes vulnerable and the penalties for going down are higher.